strata

strata

Joe Ross

DUSIE

Copyright, Joe Ross 2008.

STRATA was typeset in Adobe Garamond Pro, Arial and Market Deco.

ISBN: 978-0-6151-8823-2

First Printing, Joe Ross 2008

Non-commercial reproduction of this work is permitted and encouraged. Reproduction for profit is prohibited except by permission of the author.

Dusie Books are published by **Dusie Press**
: Dusie Press : Zürich, Switzerland :
: editor@dusie.org: http://www.dusie.org :

for Julien

STRATA

The Disappearance	15
A Riddling	16
In Fact	17
Correction	18
The Marking	19
Something Forgotten	20
Just Before	21
Directions	22
Continuation	23
In Line	24
Mass Conspiracy	25
No Title	26
Interpolation	27
Itinerant	28
5 O'Clock Shadow	29
The Sudden	30
Chosen	31
Representation	32
Procedural	33
Tuning	34
By The Way	35
Slow Going	36
Here	37
There	38
Time	39
Flow	40
Passage	41
Fault	42
Start	43
Rise	44
Permanence	45
Impermanence	46
Wish	47

Cadeau	48
Lessons	49
Secrets	50
Fable Number One	51
Pose	52
Tour	53
Waiting	54
I had a Dream	55
Gentle History	56
Exposure	57
Nice Move	58
Landing	59
As Is	60
Reverberations	61
Formation	62
Resistance	63
Evidence	64
Pacing	65
Beauty	66

"52 is some kind of magic number, isn't it?"

The Disappearance

This perfect, an act.
Resplendent palm slight of –
Gone from view, those few
we seldom thought of for fear
or its lack. A sudden not speaking
where only yesterday teased into or away
from permanence. The wheels can't
clock back, as if to fall, stall, attack.
What whether held us in breech?
My teeth gummed to the soul of want.
As a desire to deride suppositions
intent on bragging a claim. It is not so.
Is it not so?
The green shades dawn about.
Prior to night is night's call.

A Riddling

A shot, taken against its own.
Violence ceased prior to de-
cision, as if and yet each held
direction. The wind is still. Strongest
nearer the sea. Or
simpler urns to yearn for
what costs can't be contained in
unison sounding out our own doubts. Or paternity
held trundled by the very thought of posterity.
What subject? Is not a Queen's making.
This lineage begotten of desperate influence.
A choice if you will. A censure,
plague or pox.

In Fact

It wasn't a witnessed act
intent to be watched surreptitiously.
The night's obvious persuasions aloft
as fever. A centurion at the close
of some duty. What remains or whose were
born upon this brunt. Stillness
defined by the absence seen. A
screen idling as the cinders of Plato's fire.
It seems too youth has left its regrets
behind for us. Out on the prowl
a boy watches
as an ambulance goes by –
a siren, a song.

Correction

What can
can cannot hold. A declaration
absconded with prejudice. Yet
the horses are still armored
against tomorrow.
Row if row must, this contagion
taken from first land. It was
not history between she and he as
some have us believe. A new
brand, the better apple.

The Marking

A sage, blown against the pane
knocking. What knack for keeping
silence at bay. In green counted by
pallets each trapped. The need to know
versus the acceptance. This is.
Would the world not be the case?
A quick chop at the ladder. It was
a jump that got us here. Raise the flags
name the names, flail about.

Something Forgotten

The necessary infringements have
lapsed. While abutments hover into an overpass
or surplus stasis. When all is
perfect at the end of protracted need.
Will you come?
Memories seem pulled apart as if their
construction was forgotten. A fixture,
liminal, caught erasing these after thoughts. Light is here
with resilient permutations. Like we
thought. Presumptions continue striking indifference.
A dividing succession or regressive suppositions.
This description. An hour before the trees
where thinking is. A path in history.

Just Before

It lasts nearly as stone.
This light ducking as a discretion
makes way. As if choice. Or
a will to bind without being bought.
Or brought to the forefront of some
incredible yearning, as by the sea.
Outlooking is being. A sudden
stillness shimmering as a kiss. The cliffs
without description. A language.
In here you find the dogs bark
just for the joy. What would
you become from such wander? The
trees return to words.

Directions

In the silence there is no saying.
Each upon their own back. Because
there is no saying. Yet early as in
round walks or speech nearer the border,
than passage. Pressed against what correction,
correlative, rumination? This first land
trucked to appropriate dislocations.
In uniform. From such place as look –
what sleep the mind has made. Such
landscapes. Ringed with wait and a bit
or rock approaching smoke. All day in a sea
of somewhere else. The farther out of planes
of meditation or self evident revolutions.
The mind is made everywhere. There is a turn
to get back. Speech because there is no saying.

Continuation

It wouldn't have happened without
the breeze or perfect secluded intervals.
The in between of history or naming
is this disease. Disguised as knowledge
he took his seat at his table. She
had no choice but to agree. Until
they are dead and forensics becomes foreshadowing.
We hadn't the time to wait for the fruit to ripen.
Each music or something pleasurable. When forced
to respond to chains. How held
the fate is held back. The all
inclusiveness of repetition or something fought
over. Something re-begun.

In Line

Not knowing is the best state. And
privilege to be the head of it. A road map not
to be followed is what the guide said.
What is eternal is transfigurative, so
the book said. Take the nearest stairs
and wrestle with them is what I said.
For fear of being beneath weight.
This heaviness of yes, or the heaviness of no.
We divided the loaf in half.
and exactly half were left out. This is
invention. This is fable when asked.

Mass Conspiracy

Something like an economy or phrases
of speech. Words broken before backs.
This sudden starting or stopping calling history
or social, disorder. What reflected?
Any possibility without code. Frozen
in attempts or all day in the square.
A parade in perfect lock step with constructed
emotion. If will were a way. Older
outer means of control. Again the word
social. Nearer shards than bread.
The disagreement came in something
like an economy. Something or phrases
of speech in something like an economy.
Before broken words before backs.

No Title

So begin in the world of dark.
What pressured to what mirror to what motive
is you? Each examined left out. The saying goes.
The saying goes away. On the table there is a box.
And in the box is a saying some say.
It is a grand avenue. It is miniature architecture.
It is a model or a crusted bone. How long held
the disguise itself transfigures the face. It was
a flower in a box on some window one could
not look out. So begin in the world of dark.
It was a chariot rode without opposition. It had
a face for itself and a face for the mirror.
It had a name and a word for that name. It
was taken in the sun. It left no shadow.

Interpolation

And now I have a table and
an old man sitting under a tree and
some memories and finally no rules nor
name for you. How to address this. When the
knot finally slips and the world comes back.
When tomorrow correctly takes its place as today.
We began to talk but quickly chased the words away.
We put in a symbol, let it be A. It
immediately left for Not A. How to address this.
The sun was setting because an image was called for.
We opened all the bottles in our sleep. Saw straight
through the bottom. It was still dark when we awoke.
Ready for the new day in our sleep still sleeping.
How to address this, let it be Not A.

Itinerant

It was the voice that was missing.
Several who looked like you could
have been. But passed. A distance
to a photograph or planes heard
overhead. Was it caught in stride?
Out lasting is a hair's growth or very
good friends of necessity. It seemed just
a moment ago. Twin towers in battle
dividing you even farther apart. A
bridge will not do. It was something spoken
without a voice – the blue dot after
staring into sun. It wanted to be called
poetry because the voice was missing. What else
lasted assured the arrival.

5 O'clock Shadow

Frozen into near trance falling. A
cord twisted about the peace yet to be.
Singular made or a harbinger of deserted
containers. Each dusted with a way you
almost remember. Can it be so hard?
You knew the facts but I must not address you.
A legitimacy only in agreed code. I must
not be. The weakling devoured devout. A
description circumspect upon nearer light.
A certain slant of certain night. What
is avoided is the position held – What worth
brings you to me or I to you. No more
dying for what is found there. Sooner
begin to the almost lasts.

The Sudden

To complete the mosaic. Water laps
upon rocks of the scraps of sound of some
piece of photograph from the mind's memory taken.
To take to wing from a ground shaken in thought's
thought – to fill the make in make believe. The shallows
collapse. What was built upon mere sticks or the backs
of the lesser. The coal of a civilization about to be
forgotten. Forged or foreign? What ready reply.
A more gentle we or the stronger steel applied. An
older women rocking, a ship with few aboard.
The voice off water breaks. A louder call
across a divide. The light reflecting the darkness
from some surer still place. You remember.
What slipped in the holds between it and we.

Chosen

A smoke dusted across some acreage. Yet
believing the impossibility of space. What distance
between one to another or rehearsed conversations
with oneself. A stone skipped in unturned want.
Nearer leaves than far begins. Each blown
in winding stars – where hope lives its last moss.
This sand, a projection. A mountain underwater
in the early twilight of forgetting. A stenciled
weaving upon an unraveling mind or fractured
voices of a younger sun. What final peace
lies? An agenda of perfected belief or a force
feed army of salvation in hypnotic abeyance.
This cost without originals replicating, drones.
The despotic spreading or the word over the life
encountered. An easy appeal of the mass
turning mob.

Representation

In the space that is not margin how begins.
A declarative beyond position. What social
order in not knotted upon twisted spine. In flight
dreaming or the land found not taken. It was
a clear day or so the speaker said. Our attention
is bought at such a high price we can't help
but be the pursued target. What is fractured is permanent.
The sustained afterglow of persistent between. Such is
condition. A sway upon unsteady ground or figure
without frame. In a dream but with real bullets.
As if today's sponsor yelled duck, and meant it.
In cracks of subjugated persistence – a world
of cost of. The lingering fad of eventual forgetfulness
and the sudden pull of a half hoped tug.

Procedural

It was called the end because
the beginning was nowhere in sight. Such
high hopes obtained their natural quietness.
It was a trial of character with the character
absent. Or a complete dissolution of
the permanent divide and other logical
inconsistencies.   So delicious were the theorems.
A child's voice cracks but not before the adult.
We live in an age where insincerity is personal.
Believe what you want. Time had
its hands at the neck of this century, you said.
And reason very conscientiously opted out. Its
a bygone day for a bygone world but nobody
really believed that in the check out line next to
the all night daycare center.

Tuning

There is a coast, a caste
to define what shape
breaks or rules not
so much of some
as you. To be left
out or the all
between of days of rain.
It was an exercise
of exclusion, a power
curled, culled, or begotten
some called inheritance.
And yet as if, a child's genes
chosen from an unwashed pool.
The stains linger towards or
to the roof of doubt. It calls
us back, the register
of see.

By The Way

for Rae

And so I read it backwards
waiting at the gate - number,
time, destination.
Was pretext.
Waiting to dissolve itself
of else is, so small.
We read because it was
written upon a page,
or a page on
intercom, or a page at the hotel where I
forgot my case. And it is.
Upon arrival you'll leave
me waiting for a group
photo, or
relic, to forget.

Slow Going

Orange becomes us most
near sunset or in candle.
The light now so heavy rests
with purpose or interest, this will.
So clean as if to be seen in
which nearer ever of thought.
How will you be? Brought back in
an easy sail by the bay of forgetfulness.
The near or slow lack of language where once
hid brilliance like the punch of a joke.
The year's take before speech's recognition
of well earned absence. The words won't
come, or do and not connected to
memories severed link of an attachment
to all that was, all that was once
the person on the end of bed.

Here

The time, time takes so
that one waits for not
that thing. To become
one must not hesitate
but wait not too quickly
without one.
Such
as such and none too late.
The place, place one puts
is now, is ever.

There

A rush after, falls
silent in the drown of wish –
Full of memories yet
dis-connected. Hello
spun from the sudden when
all is with or without.
If you were words, & words
were want and not this,
this instead. Oh to be
that tree of sudden wood.
But can could, as you know
and all is the orchard
where I hid.

Time

The tree is not envious
for its lack of green.
Each grain holds
would not the forest come.
How to explain then?
The plain smaller silence
opening out
from the center of fall.
To be heard
definitely, deafeningly
without sound's seduction.
Each chop planted
years before in accord
with nature
is nature's
hold.

Flow

The river is brown as sound
as we know.
The rush of each morning's
fury, to be
repeated at each evening's
end, to not be
that current with which
all is heroic.
Stone block upon shoulder's
heaved, lifted and
sent back.

Passage

At intersections, or at lap —
the corners of angles
where buildings meet is pause.
it is gray pink stone
the force. Energy is vaulted
over and gone in an arch.
Such said stands
the wanting tooth's passing.
Under pillow without
thought, as if to be
but be without
is not hunger which keeps
us up or out.

Fault

Such small sound
as hard as heard
over the rumble
of being.
You before you
were
not separated to
become two.
You answer back
say, I.

Start

Impermeable is the golden
abstract as blonde.
All rest in
between each stall's failed
start. To take up
arms or to reach out.
This illusion of
outrageous fortune cast
not at liberty
but its loss.

Rise

The silhouette in perpetual
gazing. How arm
opens out. As if reach
still burning in company
of ash. You light
here with in each
other. Still dawn.
The breath heavy
as sex is light.
To return
the look of each
is other's welcome
from night.

Permanence

The frost on glass is taken
from the sign as
wood. Before wood was,
was how that each
answered back. And here
in the early yet still
morning do you come? To
reach a somewhat perceptible
yet hazy, and barely –
Why? Can thought etch
fine on the green of meadow?
The tree still there, holding
or mocking, somehow calling
your strife at where outer
reaches sky and comes –
ever so quickly
back.

Impermanence

And yet the road
grasps, slowly
its track. Through graveled
field is the in-between
where care reaches its back.
Because the cows know –
the field is green.
The rains let loose
of centuries washed. There
space. Fertile tempered
by season and those
who think lords, but
yet the rocks have their own time
and each step taken is
closer
to passing on
nothing.

Wish

Was it you?
There in the new.
Morning is a verb –
fresh outlined
the action.
Sorry, did you say
evasion or invasion?
I can't quite hear what
turned up
at the outskirts
of lasting. Remembering
peace was a verb too.
A complication necessary
and known not for
its fact but by what
it missed.

Cadeau

A rose –
bush in winter.
Vine waiting
the too obvious
wine. Wisp of . . .
The bruine of mind is
no matter how far
from the sea still
called brouillard.
Where what's covered
is the brilliance hid
in the package
you unwrap.

Lessons

Description ends
in an open field, where
you learned to speak.
The grasp grows
but slowly on and on.
So droll this role
where what's wrapped,
is bound, borrowed, & found
sorely lasting.

Secrets

for Buck

If this were
simply found
words on
scrap.
Papers passed
between
friends who call
and their lack.
I would weep –
but not for
beauty who
does not need
such help.
But help us
beauty if we
you lack.

Fable Number One

There was one time
that time thought
was once upon a motion
now lost. It flees
so fast. One
wonders one
doubts if
words held ever
what this (hi)story
missed. If ever held
words. Where ever
ever had lived as never
never grounded.

Pose

In the dark of sculpture
the cutouts hold light
to the chin
firmly planted forward.
It is
twisted sex
leading face first into form.
As if that photo rose
to snap shut its pose
and you caught from all sides of skin
peeled back fruit
from the table still.
And yet you held the motion
firmly in teeth, between the bits
the bite so delicious

Tour

for Andrew Zawacki

Perhaps the stag.
Perhaps the doe.
In night perhaps the night.
What sack drops its contents
in spring blooms shoot
into each failing.
The mother
ducks into round
up what follows
came before. Each be
is met in its opposite's
approach. Is its shadow
from necessary light.
From necessary light
we stare into, where
we came, where we go (return).

Waiting

A cigar in the park
parmi les deux arbres -
makes sense.
Entre le bois sans bruit.
Il n'y a pas de choix.
It was you – Je n'étais pas
and yet past holds
only a frame – A word/sound
is a sound/word emptied of its meaning.
Vas-y, il n'y a pas de choix.
Entre les deux arbres
Parmi la nuit et des journées
we kick around smoke
not far from ash
Vas-y, il n'y a pas de choix.

I Had a Dream

for America

Heavy heels on wood
sounding so
in-elegant in hoes.
The world knows
what will follow
is not the lead nor
leaden match
that ignites the flame
of a torch not free
to stand for any nor
one united or not.
The bell cracks
where once sounded
hope. Liberty is hell
bound between freedom
strikes. And in the tower
it is neither one if, nor two if
but is what if, what if . . .

Gentle History

Today's dream is
tomorrow
revved up with
too many
places yet to go.
Just like a bowl of rice
she said it best
to clean after the hunger
is steam. Where you wait
after the rain was a part time
law on the road taken
though if you are able to think
at all, well good for you
and your syllables. But I think
that you are sound, as sound
as stone is sound
before music
as sound
as sleep.

Exposure

A photo from scaffold
hung by a man
around the neck with cement.
You ask the older woman
to snap it first.
This is your souvenir
of this park even though
it was posed. So you had no choice
answered back,
smile.

Nice Move

It there were to be reason
in the rhythms
or vibes in the vie,
you would be
no sooner close
to that which you
will become, before you
had made it back
and opened out
of step
into extinction or
exultation of that
which you call
grace.

Landing

Time is
this place destiny's
calling out to
inner longing's completed
image. Of course,
she said run.
And dare to be
out of step
or out of tune's
mind. There/where you
come.

As Is

A voice is a sound
from far away closer.
As a child's sneeze
begs the question of being.
How far apart, the eyes
see in stereo as sharp
as focus is closer lost.
The thing held
cannot be fully,
retrieved as falls
leaves burning a new
reminds one of what's to come,
has already been done.
It is difference, defiance –
this dating carbon into
diamond's rough.

Re-Verberations

Friend from far away
begin to chase distance
nearer to be –
longing or not.
Your flag waves
each stride's closer
to step. If this
house had a roof
perhaps the rain
wouldn't be
so wet or so fast.
And what of
choice, or the illusion
of? An allusion
of a mirage in a mirror
mistakenly taken
as you.

Formation

Here the different
colors of brown
mean something sure.
It is not old
or dirty. But just the same
the checks become plaid,
pale, and unopening onto
anything you've mis-taken
as yours. It is a question
of ownership. As if flowers
shoot into a sweeping broom.
It's not said, how the flow
resembles its interruption.
One takes paddle, bending
just beyond sight.

Resistance

All in a row
the men sit
in the last fading
of autumn's light.
They know
the sun is only as
sunny as them.
When the light shows
another -
war breaking before dawn,
we remember not
the peace but
the rest.

Evidence

They stop to seem to stare
at a photograph
in which I am not.
There, the old man with
a white Chinese beard. What
does he say of frames? She
wears a long black coat opened
to the wind. Perhaps it is the shoes.
That I can't forget that description
is narrative and color never helps.
The pause is gaze inside out passing
as we move chairs into the sun.
The children try to help and
speak loudly in simple words.

Pacing

The water falls in buckets
of forgetfulness as certain
as evidence matches time.
On this square, geometry means
nothing simply.
So the passers-by do, all of which
is very pleasing.
To go without a plan on horseback
takes a day and
sets the limit of meaning.
What grows from evolves at best
naturally, but that is best left
unsaid.
It is perhaps miraculous
this reflection from a puddle
in the mirror running backwards.

Beauty

These layers measure not
the depth nor define
what is left when
the surface thins
to a point
of bleeding.   Is it truly
easier to breathe
in the leaves? Looking out
into the next break, we pause.
Frozen into stare, the eye cannot help
see itself.

Laura Wilber, 2008

About the Author

Author of ten books of poetry, Joe Ross was born in Pennsylvania and graduated magna cum laude from the Honors Program at Temple University in Philadelphia. He soon moved thereafter to Washington, D.C. where he wrote his first book, *Guards of the Heart*, consisting of four plays written in poetic form.

In Washington D.C., he worked at The John F. Kennedy Center for the Performing Arts and was extraordinarily active in the cultural scene of that city. He served as the President of the Board of the Poetry Committee at The Folger Shakespeare Library from 1994-1997 and as the Literary Editor of the arts bi-monthly The Washington Review from 1991-1997. He also Co-founded and directed the In Your Ear poetry reading series at the District of Columbia Arts Center.

In 1997 he moved to San Diego, where he worked for The City of San Diego Commission's for Arts and Culture. In 1999, he left that position to put his poetics into practice, and to work directly in politics. He served as the Senior Chief of Policy for several elected officials. He also continued to be very active in the San Diego cultural scene, serving as a board member of the San Diego Art Institute and Co-founding and curating the *Beyond the Page* reading series in that city.

In 1997 he received a National Endowment for the Arts Fellowship Award for his poetry. He presently resides in Paris.

Acknowledgements:

Versions of some of these poems have appeared in *An Avec Sampler, Crayon, Green Integer Review, Job's Horse, New Review of Literature, Nth Position, Rhizome, The Germ, Tinfish,* and *Upstairs at Duroc.*

Selected poems from this book appeared in a bilingual English/Italian edition as *STRATI,* La Camera Verde Press, Rome, 2007

Many thanks to the editors, contributors, readers, and supporters of those publications.

Note:
The author wishes to extend his heartfelt gratitude to Guy Bennett whose questioning of place, geography, and relation served as the impetus for this work. Thank you, Guy.

ALSO by Joe Ross

Guards of the Heart: Four Plays (Sun & Moon Press, 1990)
How to Write; or, I used to be in love with my jailer (Texture Press, 1992)
An American Voyage (Sun & Moon Press, 1993)
Push (Leave Books, 1994)
De-flections (Potes & Poets Press, 1994)
Full Silence (Upper Limit Music Press, 1995)
The Fuzzy Logic Series (Texture Press, 1996)
The Wood Series (Seeing Eye Books, 1997)
EQUATIONS =equals (Green Integer Press, 2004)
Strati (Bi-lingual Italian/English, La Camera Verde, 2007)

DUSIE PRESS BOOKS

Elizabeth Treadwell. *Cornstarch Figurine* 2006
Logan Ryan Smith, *The Singers*, 2007
Robyn Art, *The Stunt Double in Winter*, 2007
Joe Ross, *Strata*, 2008
Kristy Bowen, *In the Bird Museum*, 2008
jen mccreary, *: ab ovo :* 2008
anne blonstein, *the butterflies and the burnings*, 2008

forthcoming

jen hofer, **laws**
Arielle Guy, ***Three Geogaophies:*** *A Milkmaid's Grimoire*
Nicole Mauro, *The Contortions*

*please direct all queries to: editor@dusie.org   www.dusie.org

www.ingramcontent.com/pod-product-compliance
Lightning Source LLC
Chambersburg PA
CBHW031209090426
42736CB00009B/846